CHRIS GOYETTE

Teddy
the Turkey's First Christmas

Trafford PUBLISHING® www.trafford.com

North America & international
toll-free: 1 888 232 4444 (USA & Canada)
phone: 250 383 6864 ♦ fax: 812 355 4082

TEDDY THE TURKEY'S FIRST CHRISTMAS

Teddy came into our lives many years ago. Aunt Cherrie and Uncle Mario had driven all the way from Oregon to stay with Auntie Cathie for the holidays to a small farm in Northern California for the Christmas dinner.

Teddy was a strikingly handsome bird. When they arrived Teddy stepped out of the car, filled his chest with the cool morning air, he stretched out his wings and ruffled his feathers. Teddy was a sight to behold. He felt so good he began to gobble, gobble, gobble. Oh what a sight to behold.

Teddy began to gobble, gobble, and gobble He let everyone within ear shot know he had arrived. His personality was so unique, friendly and loving and soon everyone forgot Christmas was only days away.

The family and other animals on the small farm soon got to know him as a beautiful bird he became part of the family and Auntie Cathie decided to name him Teddy, and he finally found a home.

Teddy became best friends with Peeper's the duck. They went everywhere together. The two of them soon joined Rommel the big German Shepherd who was like a police man protected the family and animals from the wild animals that lived in the area.

A big yellow school bus stopped at the end of the driveway, the door opens and out jumps a little boy, who come running up the driveway, the dog barks, the duck quacks. "Who's that "says Teddy." It's Tony and the dog and duck start running down the driveway to meet him. Getting off the big yellow bus running up the driveway, saw for the first time.

Later that afternoon, Teddy the turkey and Peepers the duck strolled around the pool to the home of Mr. and Mrs. Chicky the chicken family.

The Chicky's children were outside playing. Teddy said hello, and he and Peepers walked up the path. The Chicky's children ran inside their house, screaming, "Papa, there is a stranger outside."" Oh," Peppers said, "the Chicky children have been taught not to talk to strangers. "Soon after, Mr. Chicky came running out of the house," oh it's you Peepers," Mr. Chicky said, and who is this stranger'? "Well" said Peepers.

"I would like to introduce you to Teddy. He just arrived with Auntie Cherrie and Uncle Mario from the state of Oregon and is going to live here." "Nice to meet you", said Mr. Chicky, "nice to meet you said" Teddy.

Teddy thought what a good lesson it was to teach children not to speak to strangers.

As they stood th talking, Mrs. Chicky came out of the house with a loaf of fresh bread and handed it to Teddy "Welcome to the neighborhood," she said as she handed it to him. "Thank you very much," Teddy said "it smells wonderful."

Teddy and Peepers went back to Teddy's home to sample the bread Mrs. Chicky had made. "It sure tastes good", Peepers said as he took a bite. Mrs. Chicky must be a good cook, "Teddy said as night time came, Teddy stretched and yawned.

" I'm tired too," said Peepers "Thank you Peepers for such a wonderful day," said Teddy. "My pleasure "said Peepers" and tomorrow I will introduce you to some more of my friends."As Peepers left, waving good bye, Teddy thought how nice it was to have a friend like him. He crawled into bed and soon was fast asleep.

The next morning as the sun came up over the mountains and peaked thru the window, Teddy sat up in bed and could smell the fresh coffee coming from the big house. As he looked out the window he saw a man coming out the house to get into a shiny red truck, and drive away. "That must be the farmer that lives in the big house.

"I'll introduce myself to him when he gets home tonight." Teddy was about to fall back to sleep when he heard a loud noise. He got up and looked out the window. This time he saw Auntie Cathie with one foot out the door.

Suddenly Rommel ran past her barking. "ShSh Rommel, "she said, "you'll wake everyone up." I'm sorry," he said, I'll try to more quiet". Teddy was so excited to meet Rommel that he ran out the door just, as Rommel was dashing by. CRASH, "gobble, gobble, gobble" said Teddy, "Ruff, Ruff,Ruff" said Rommel, "nice to meet you." "I'm sorry "Teddy said, I didn't see you coming."I'm sorry too, said Rommel."

"I was looking forward to meeting all the other animals," Teddy said. Well they both thought it was so funny they sat there laughing. After Teddy straightened his feathers and Rommel combed his hair, And Rommel asked Teddy if he would like to go with him to the barn. "I want you to meet Mr. Fad-Eagle the horse and his family. Together they ran to the barn.

Rommel said, "This is Teddy." "I know," said Mr., Fad-Eagle, every talking about you for days now. "Nay,Nay to meet you", said Mr. Fad-Eagle, Come a little closer, "let me get a better look at you" said Mr., Fat-Eagle.
As Teddy started to walk a little closer, Rommel said," what happened to your glasses? Mr. Fad-Eagle? "

"Well," he said," I broke them playing chase with the children. "That's right," said Mrs. Fad-Eagle, sticking her head out of the barn. The children were always running around, whoosh, whoosh, be careful Sarahzad and Jazmeen, "Mrs. FadEagle said you almost knocked Teddy down."Sorry"said Sarahzad, "me too said Jazmeen," "as they ran down the meadow. They sure have a lot of spirit," Teddy said. "Oh yes,' said Mrs. Fad-Eagle, "they love to play games all day long.

"They never want to do their school work, "said Mr. Fad-Eagle, "all they want to do is run, run, run."

It was almost dinner time so easy and Rommel said goodbye to Mr. and Mrs. Fad-Eagle and started to walk down the path towards Teddy's new home. "I'm a little tired," said Teddy, "it's been quite a day."" I'm tired too," said Rommel as he stretched. "I think I'll go home and have dinner and go to bed." "Goodnight, "said Teddy, as he yawned, "see you in the morning", Rommel said.

Teddy crawled into bed and dreamed of the new friends he had met and soon he was fast asleep.

The next day was Christmas and all the family and friends started arriving for the celebration. Uncle Buddy, Auntie Andrea and Jaime arrived early in the day. Next came Julie, Caren, Marc, and Auntie Christie, who arrived at noon.

Teddy couldn't believe all the cars. Everyone was honking their horns and waving their arm as they drove up the hill. "Hi Auntie Cathie" everyone said.

By that afternoon everyone had arrived and unpacked their clothes. Teddy was so excited about meeting the rest of the family. He especially wanted to meet the little dark hair girl who has walked past his window on the way into the big house. He thought she was so beautiful.

Soon everyone sat down at the table. As dinner was served, Auntie Cathie asked, "where is Teddy," he is the guest of honor.

"Everyone looked round but Teddy was not in the house. I wonder where he is," said Rommel as he got off the chair. " I'll go get him." So Rommel went to Teddy's home and knocked on the door, "what are you doing in there?" he said. "Oh" Teddy said, just fixing myself up." He wanted to look his best, so he picked out his prettiest feather jacket.

Out came Teddy, all dressed up. "My goodness" said Rommel. "Why are you wearing such fancy clothes? "Today I saw the most beautiful dark haired angel and I want to look my best. "Oh," said Rommel.

The next day after breakfast Peepers took Teddy to the pasture to meet Freckles the cow and her little calf.. "Nice to meet you Freckles" said Teddy" and what a cute little calf you have. "thank you" Freckles said. After Teddy and Peepers and Frecklss and went back to the big house.

Teddy saw Jaime again and thought he would follow her all over the farm. Teddy gave the family lots of love, cheer and consideration for others, and, that is what Christmas is all about.

www.ingramcontent.com/pod-product-compliance
Lightning Source LLC
Chambersburg PA
CBHW060856270326
41934CB00002B/161